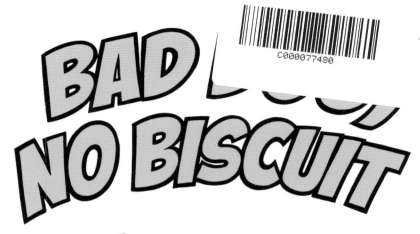

BAD DUCK NO BISCUIT

By
Anthony Smith

Souvenir Press

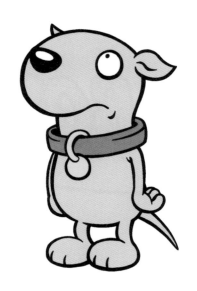

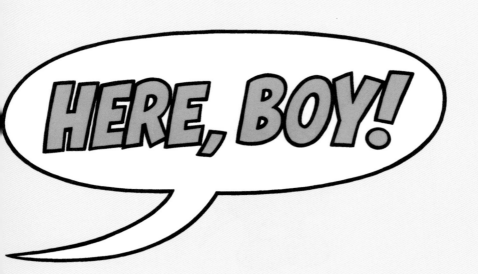

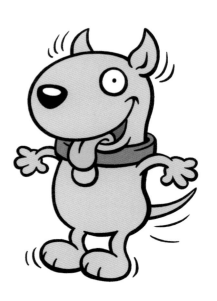

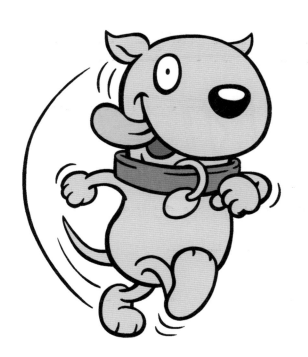

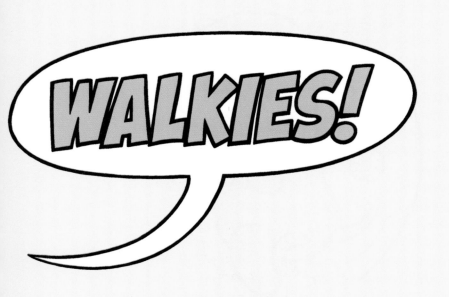

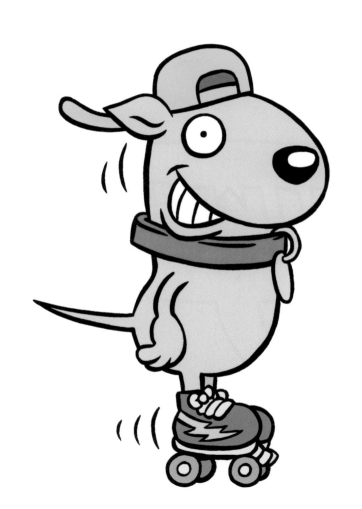

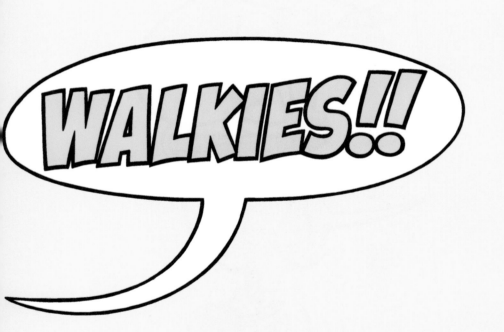

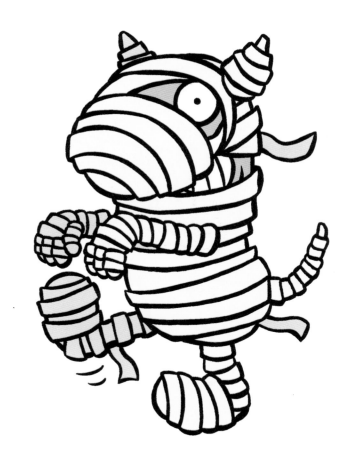

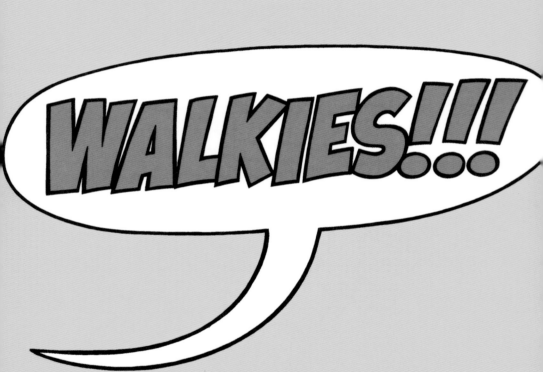

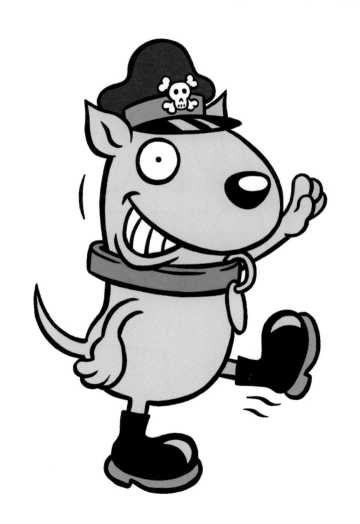

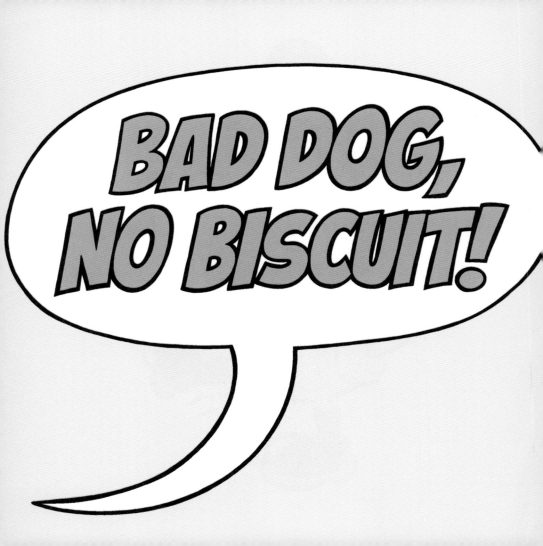

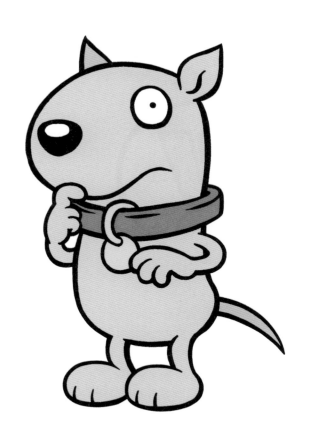

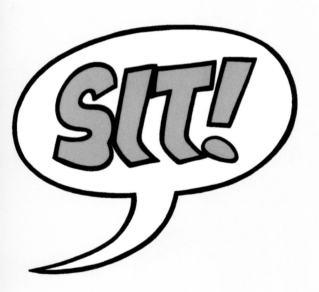

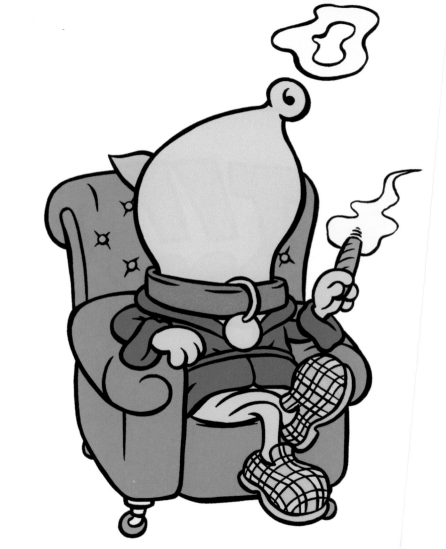

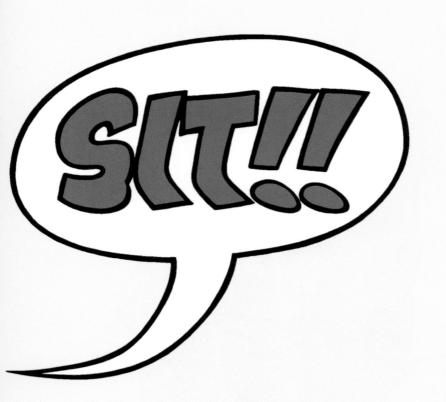

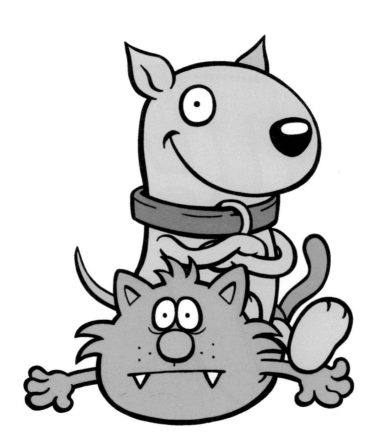

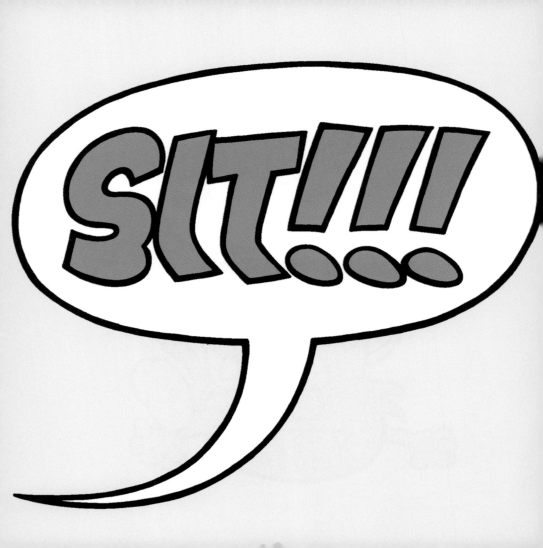

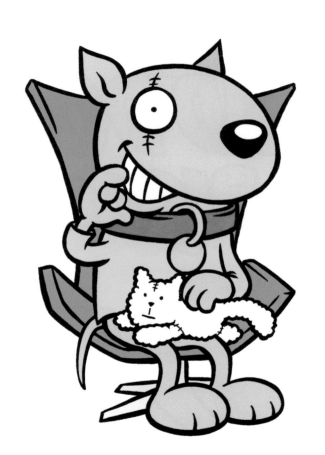

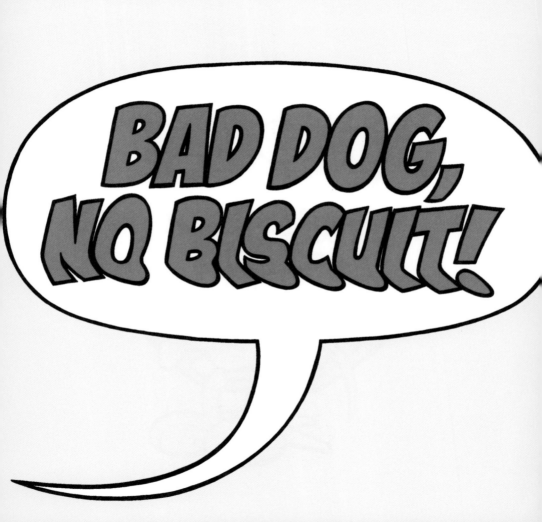

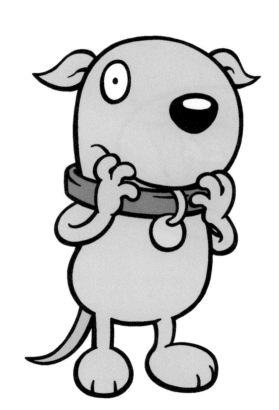

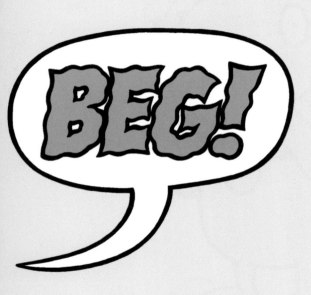

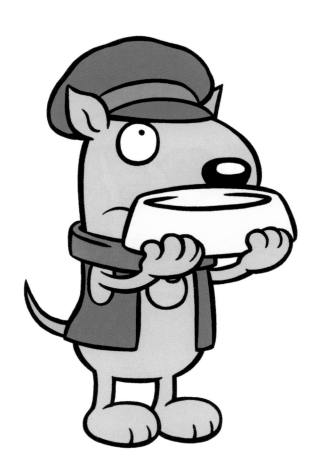

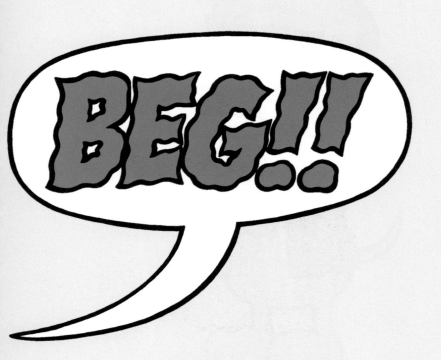

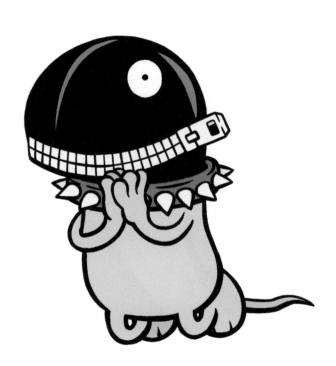

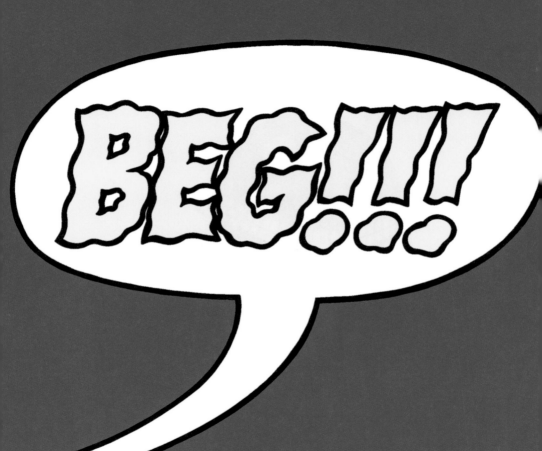

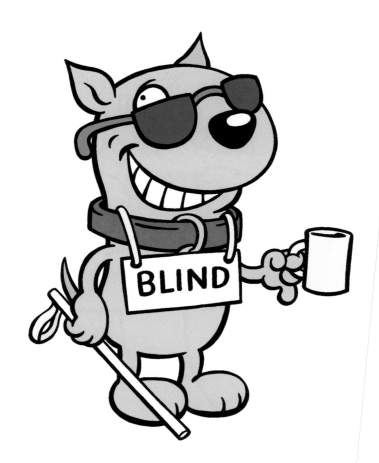

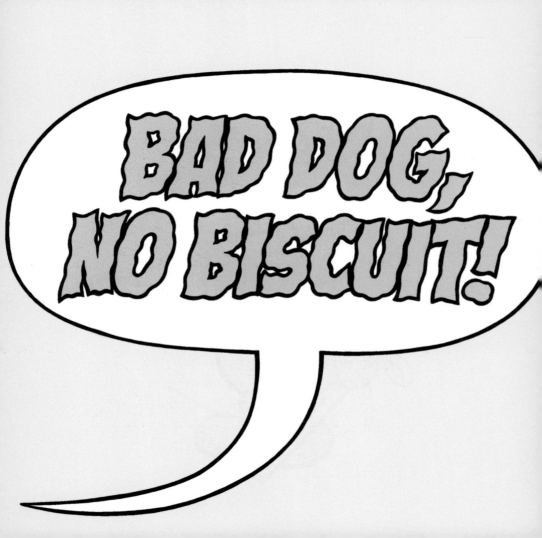

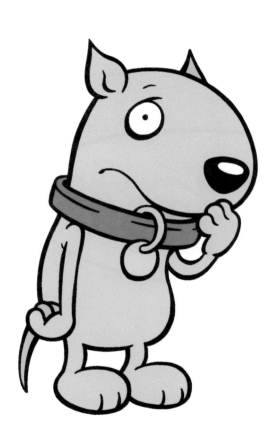

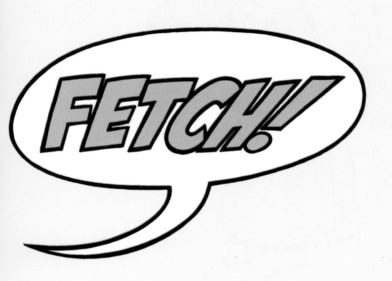

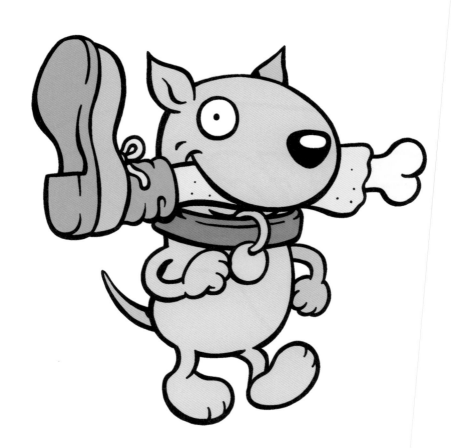

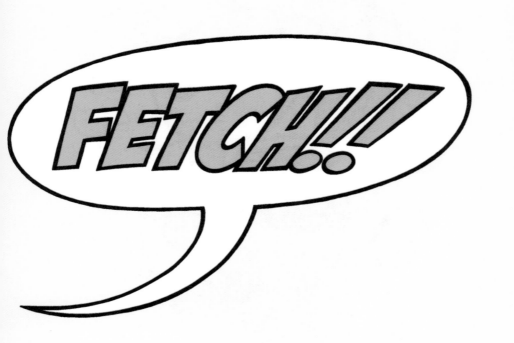

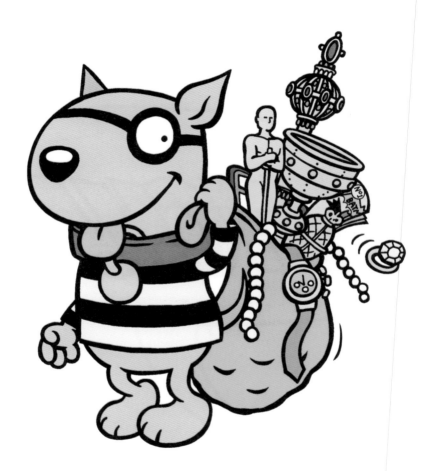

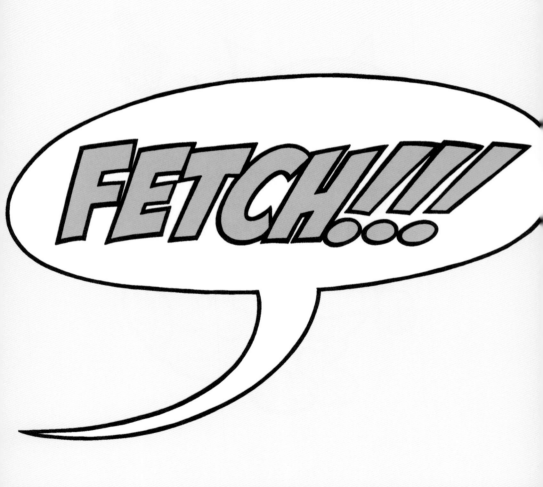

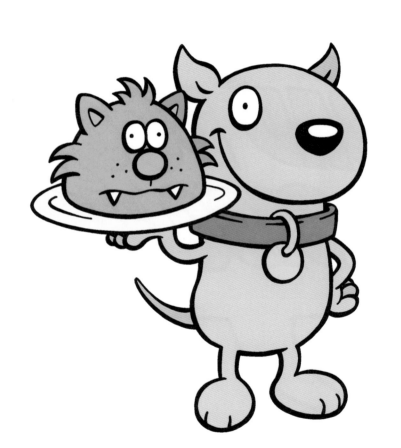

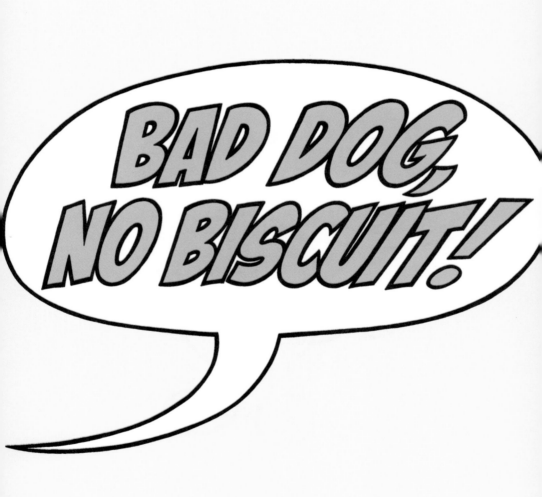

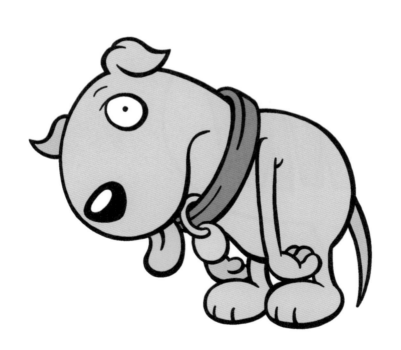

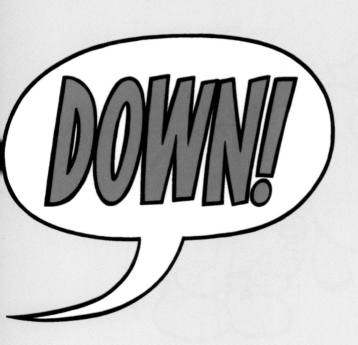

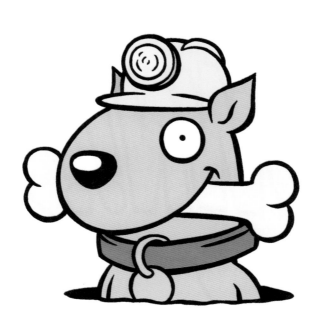

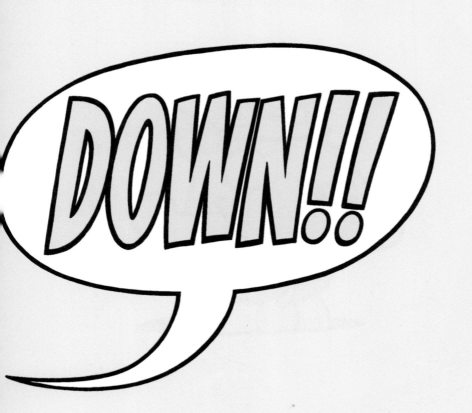

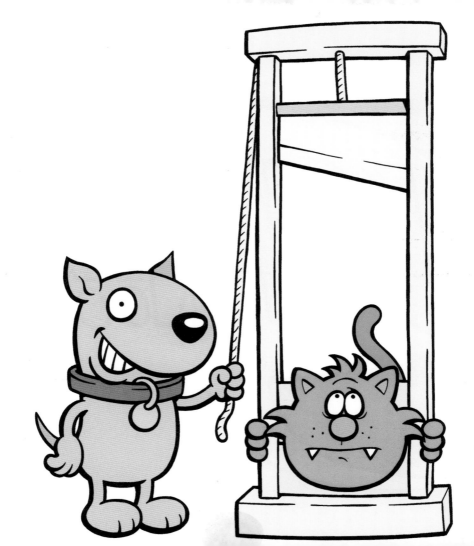

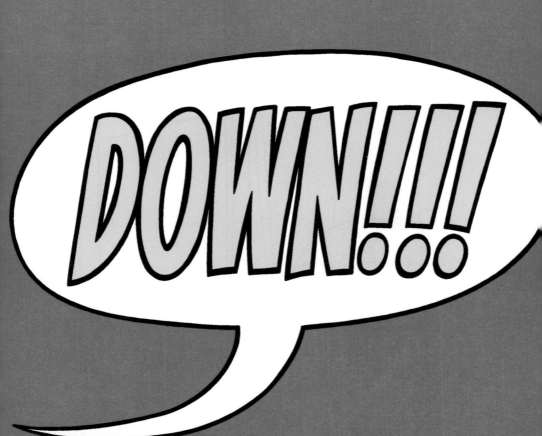

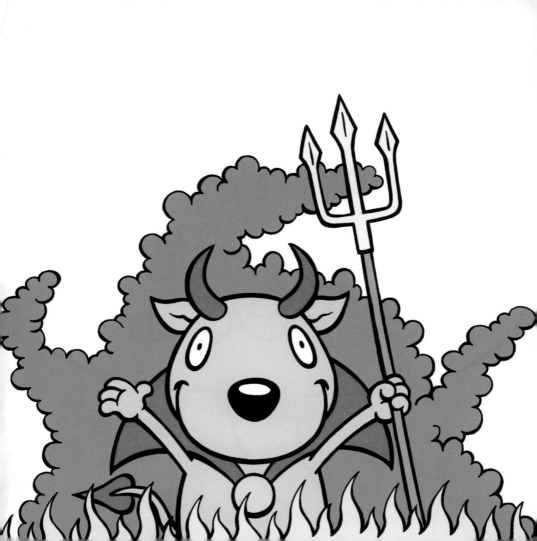

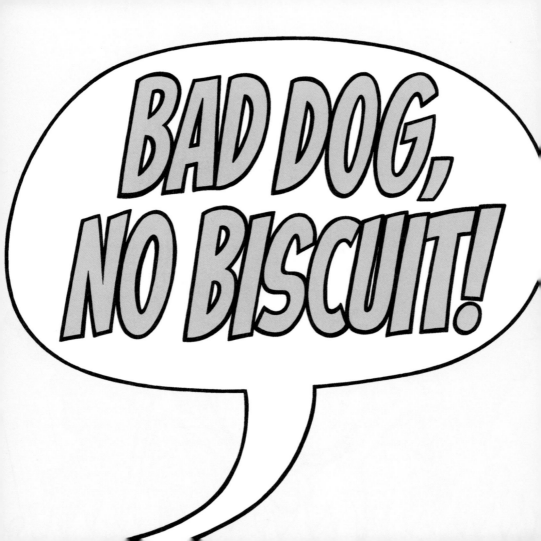

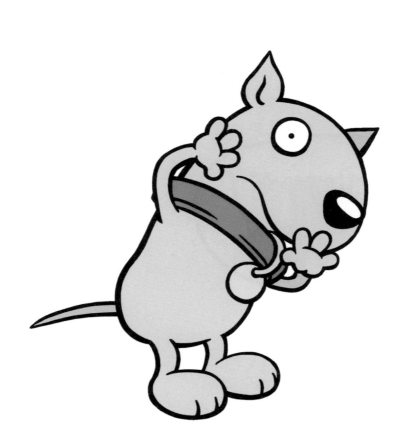

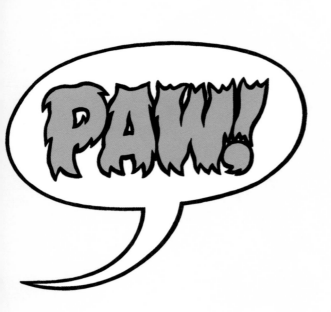

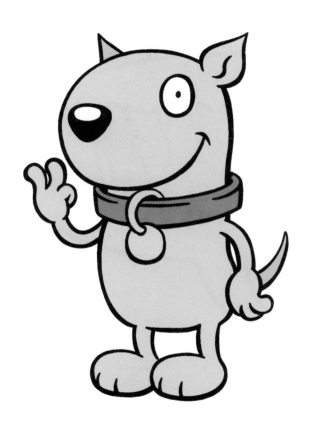

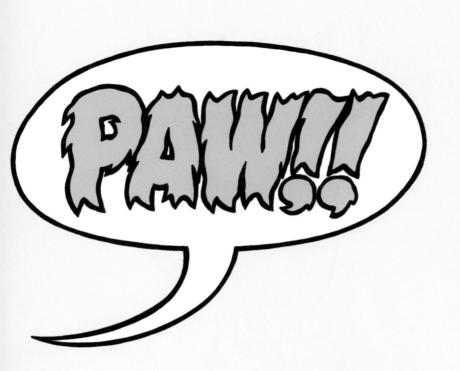

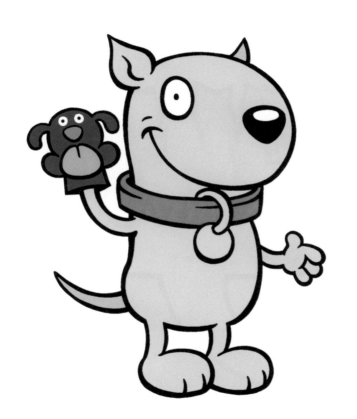

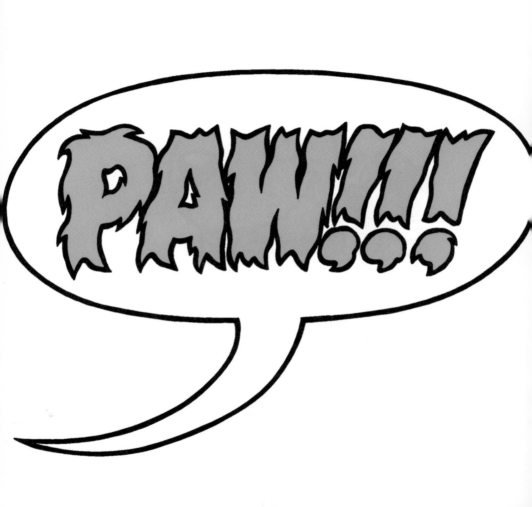

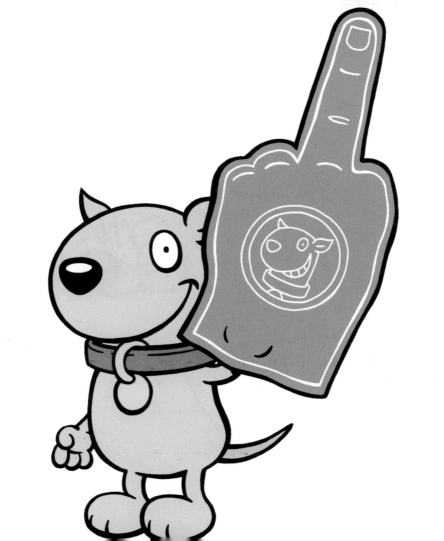

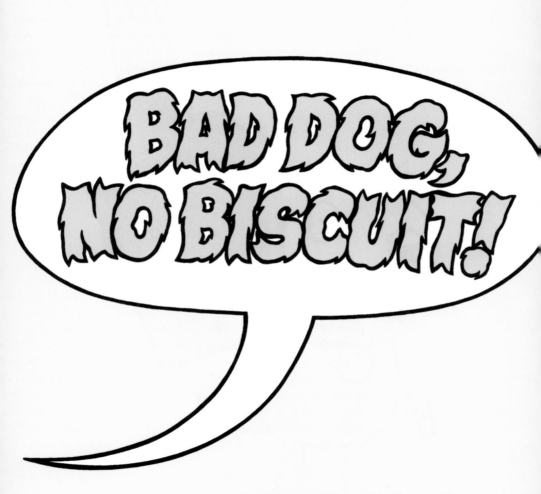

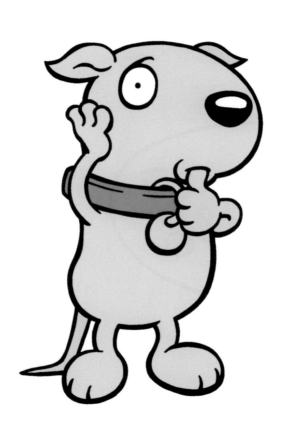

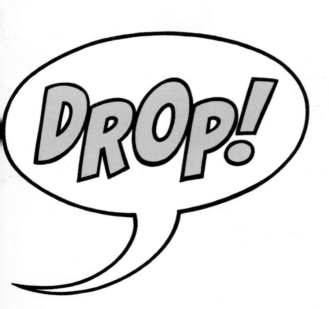

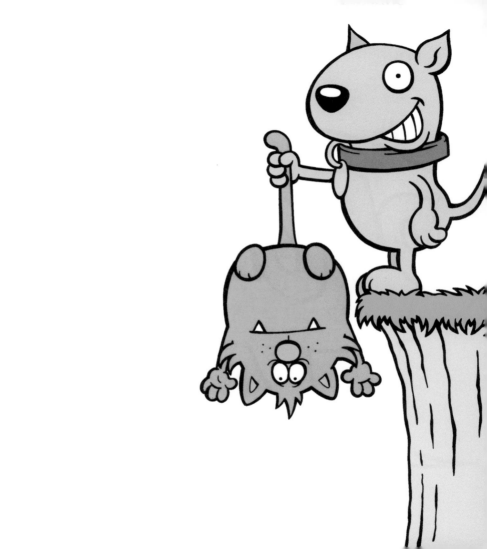

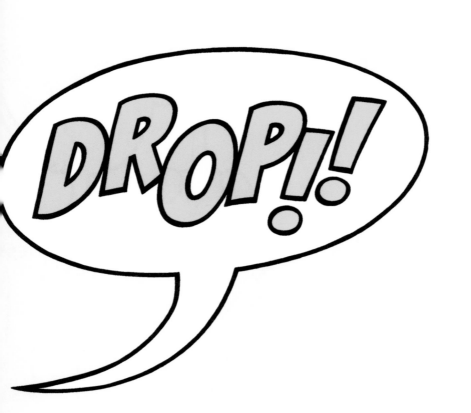

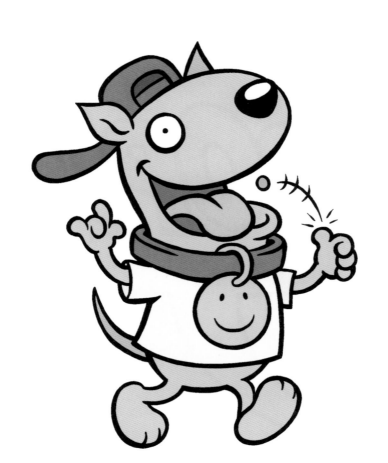

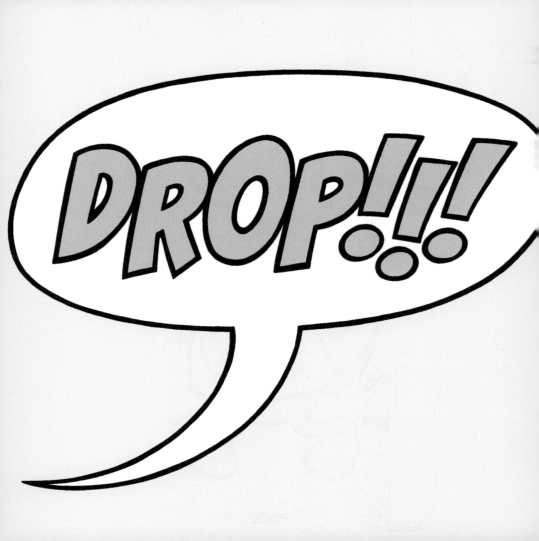

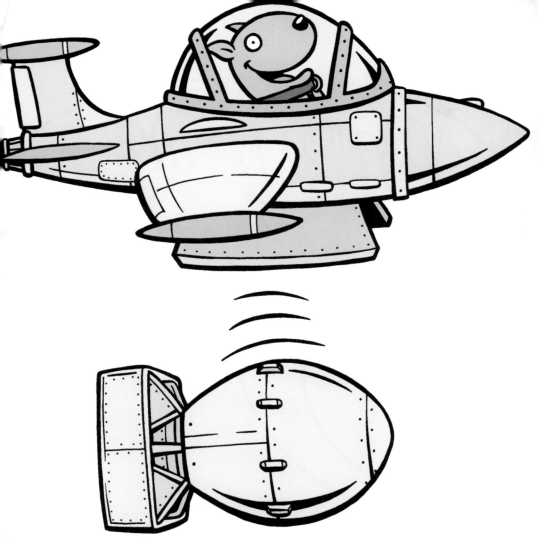

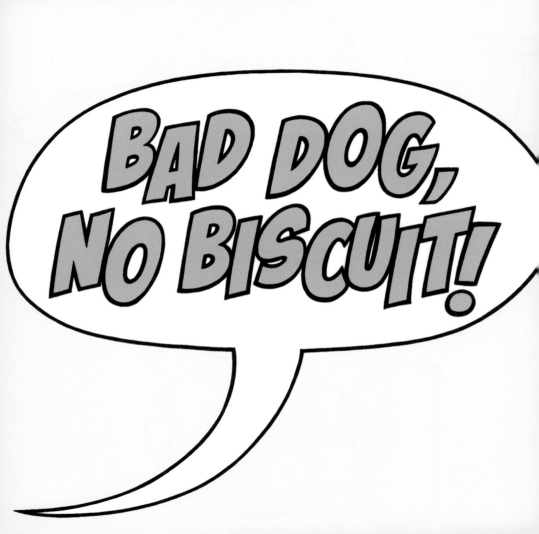

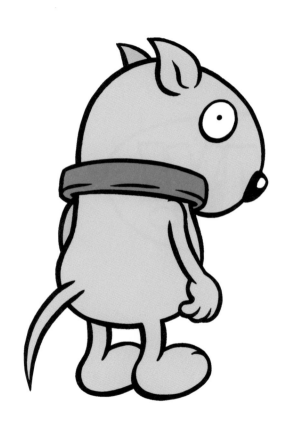

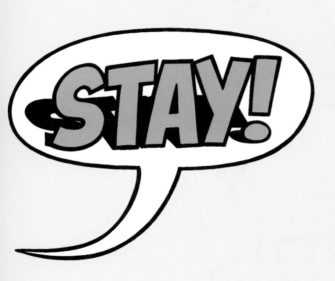

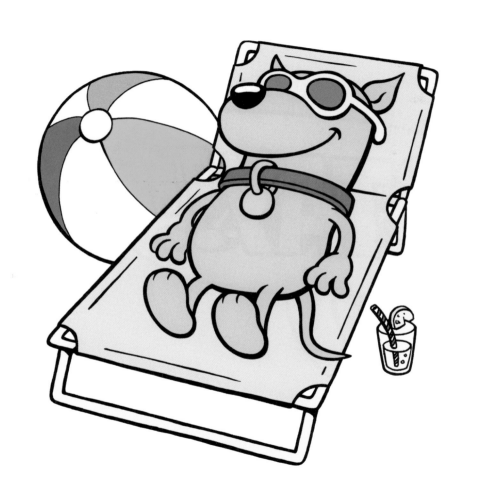

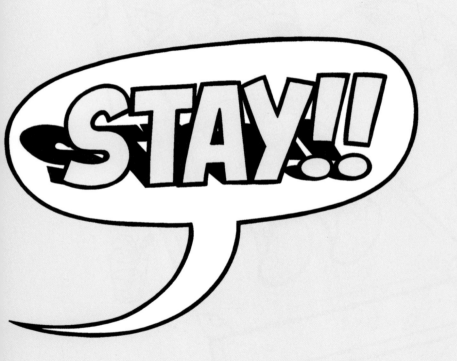

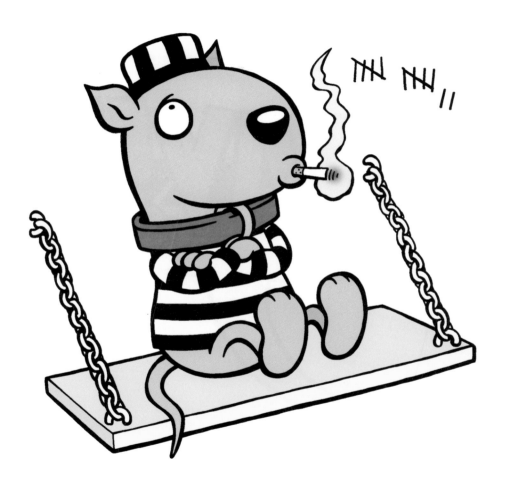

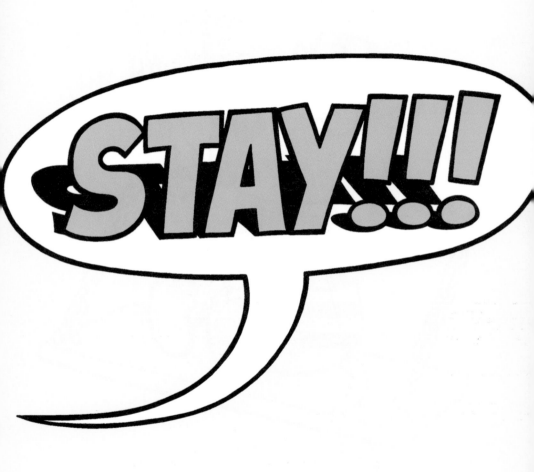

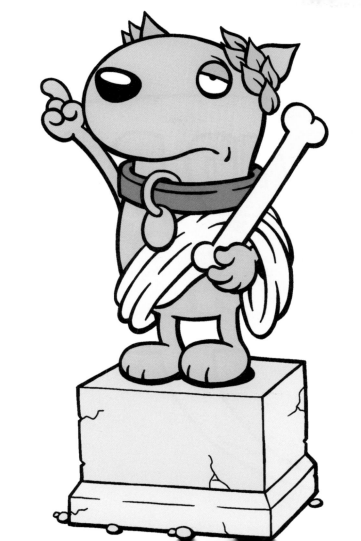

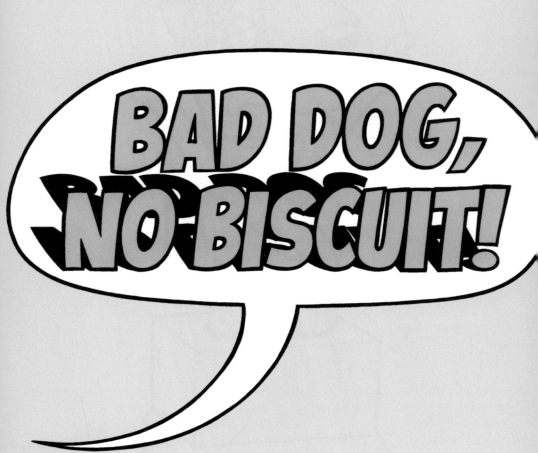

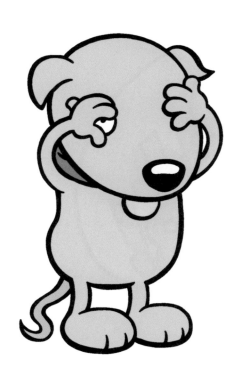

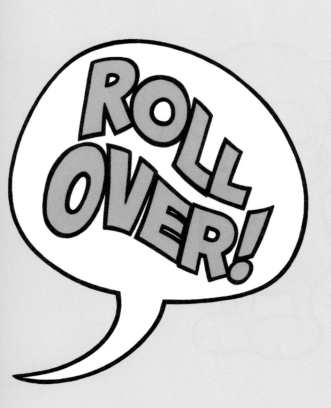

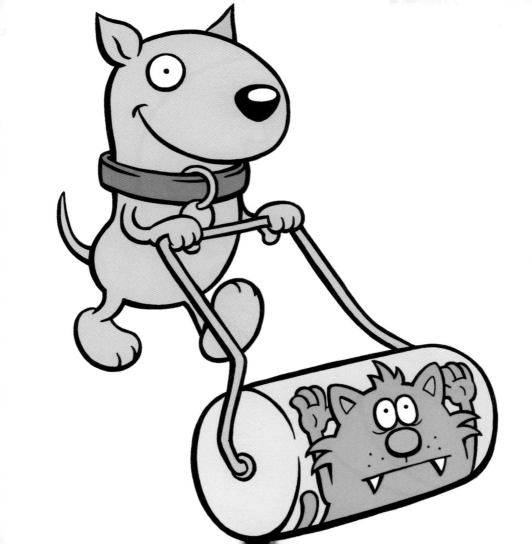

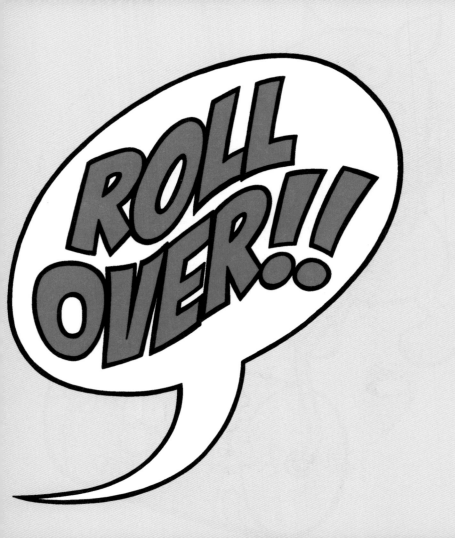

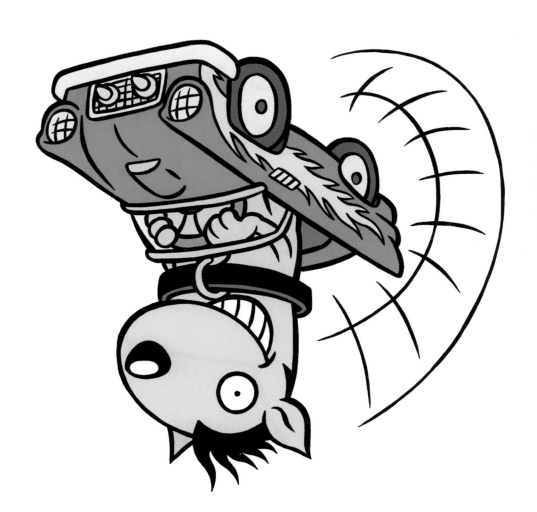

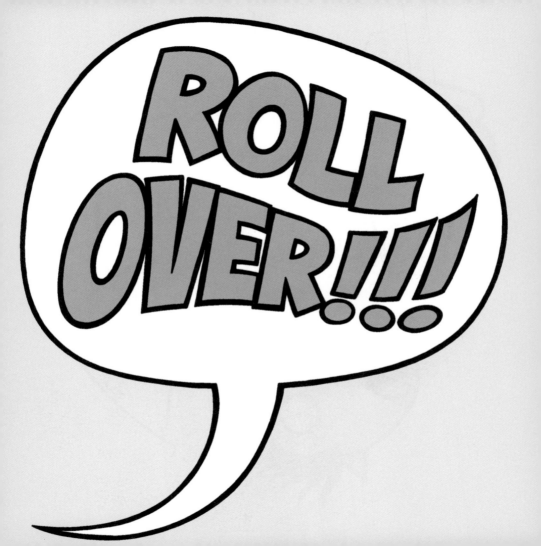

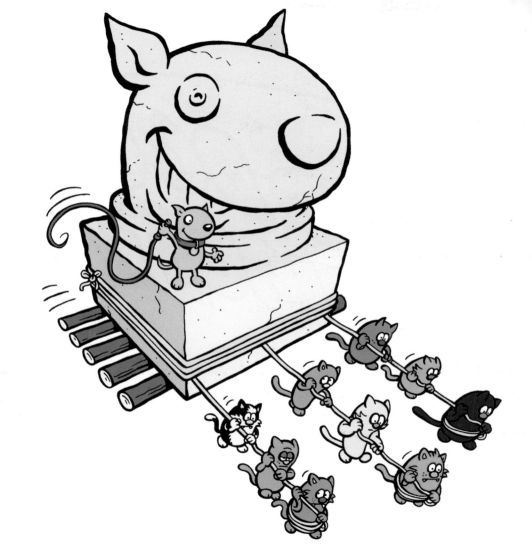

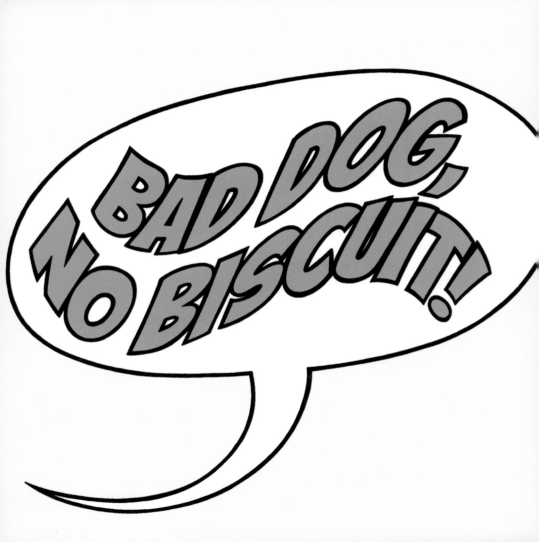

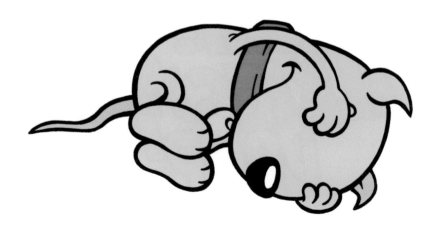

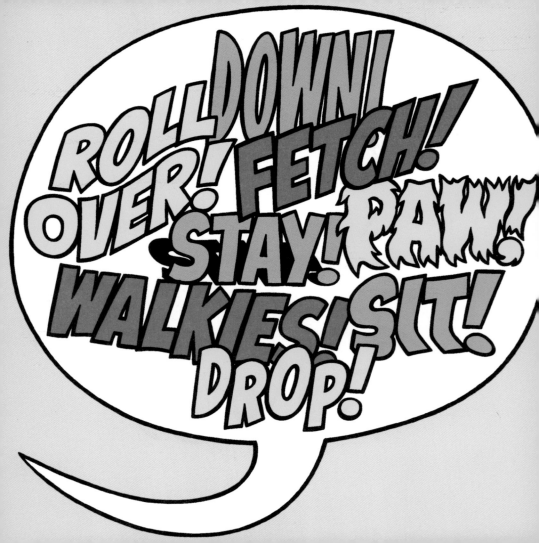

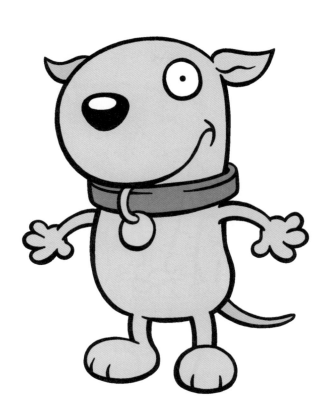

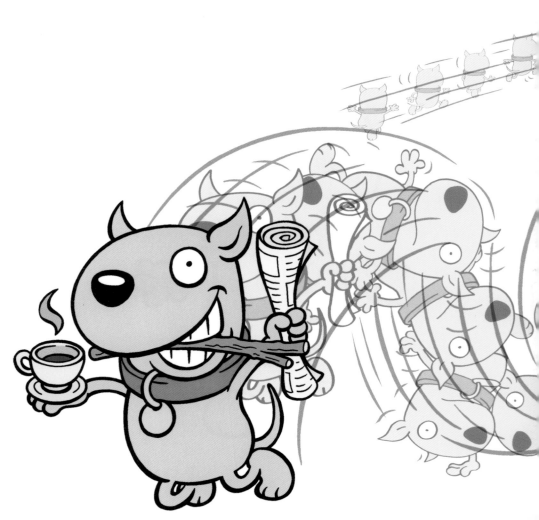

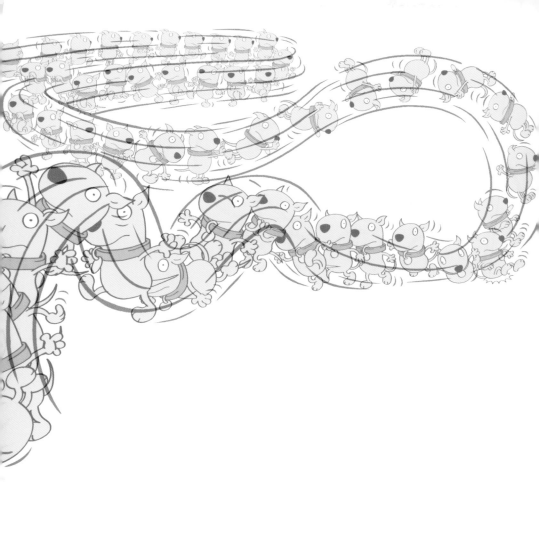

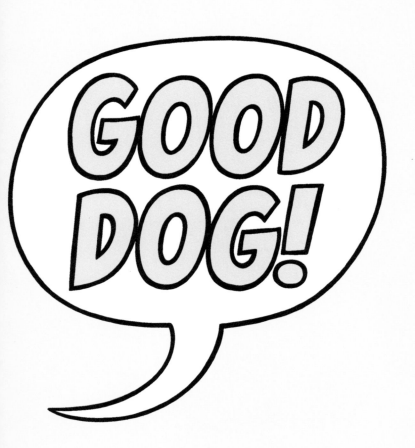

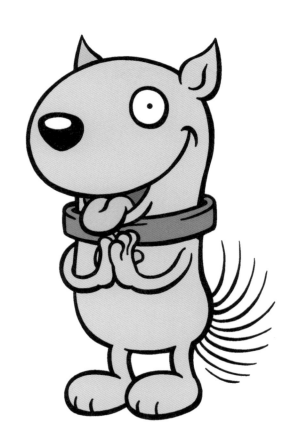

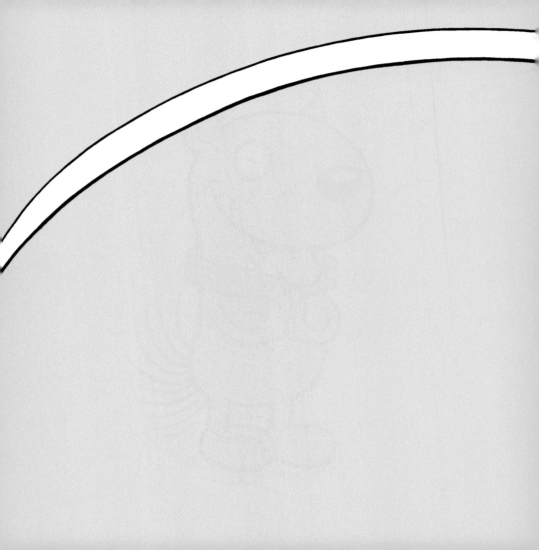

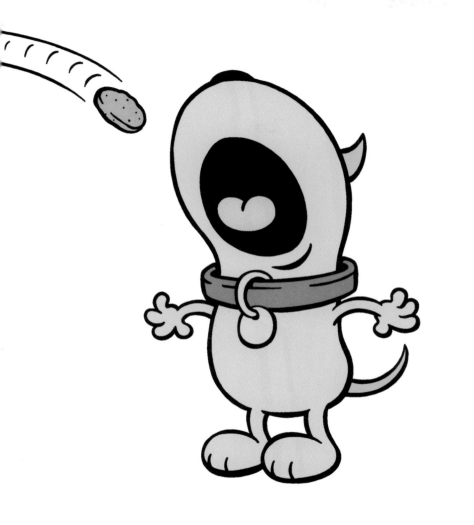

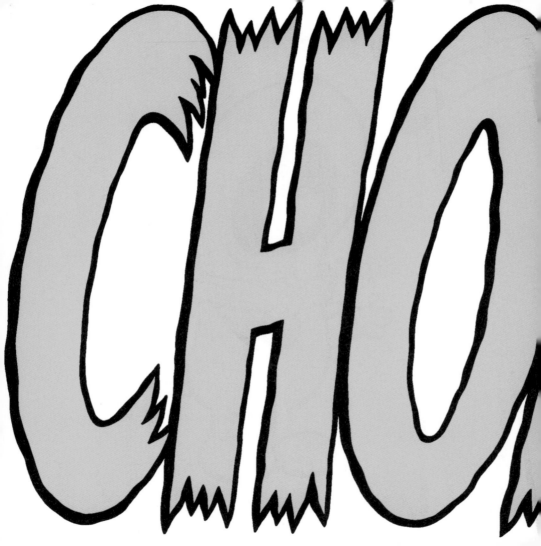

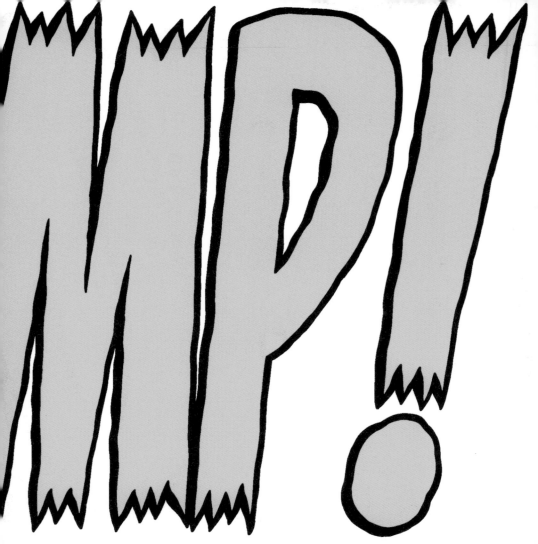

First published in Great Britain in 2013 by Souvenir Press Ltd
43 Great Russell Street, London WC1B 3PD

ISBN 9780285642218

Printed and bound in Great Britain
by Bell & Bain Ltd, Glasgow